Sue R. Brandt

Facts About the Fifty States

A FIRST BOOK I SECOND REVISED EDITION
FRANKLIN WATTS
NEW YORK I LONDON I TORONTO I 1988

FOR

RONALD, A CALIFORNIAN

MICHAEL, A COLORADAN

CHARLES, A NEW YORKER

GINNY BEL, RUSSELL, AND RODDY—
ALL MISSOURIANS

Material on the origin of state names is used by permission
from *Webster's Third New International Dictionary*, copyright
1981, by the G. & C. Merriam Company, publishers of the
Merriam-Webster dictionaries.

Maps and diagrams by Vantage Art, Inc.

Photographs courtesy of: NASA, p. 4; Library of Congress: pp. 16 (top), 17
(top), 18 (top), 20, 70; N.Y. Convention & Visitors Bureau: p. 17 (bottom);
Washington Convention and Visitors Bureau: p. 33; Arizona Office of
Tourism Photo: p. 39; Idaho Tourism; pp. 40, 52; California Office of
Tourism: p. 49; Alissa Greenberg. p. 62.

Library of Congress Cataloging-in-Publication Data

Brandt, Sue R.
Facts about the 50 states.

(A First book)
Includes index.
Summary: Answers questions on the geography, population, history, products, and many other aspects of the
fifty states.
1. United States—Description and travel—Juvenile
literature. 2. Children's questions and answers.
[1. United States—Description and travel. 2. Questions
and answers] I. Title. II. Title: Facts about the fifty
states.
E169.04.B73   1988   973'.076   87-25437
            ISBN 0 531-10476-1

Contents

Do You Know? States Trivia

How many of the following questions can you answer now? All of the answers are in this book.

1. About how far would you go if you traveled across the United States from the Atlantic Ocean to the Pacific Ocean?
2. What is the official name of the United States?
3. Is Washington, D.C., the capitol of the United States, or is it the capital?
4. Why is Delaware known as the First State?
5. Which state is smallest in area (size)?
6. Which state is largest in area?
7. What state has the longest name?
8. Which state has the largest population?
9. Which one has the smallest population?
10. What country once owned Alaska?
11. Where could you stand in four states all at once?
12. When was the bicentennial (200th anniversary, or birthday) of the United States celebrated?
13. When was the bicentennial of the Constitution of the United States celebrated?
14. Which state was once an independent kingdom?
15. What mountain peak is the highest point in the fifty states?
16. What states have "North" or "South" as part of their names?

The shape of the United States land mass can be seen at the center, through the cloud cover, in a NASA photograph taken during the Apollo 16 space mission.

17. What states have "New" as part of their names?
18. Which one of the national parks is the oldest?
19. Why is Colorado known as the Centennial State?
20. What four states call themselves commonwealths?
21. Which is farther—from the Mississippi River to the Atlantic Ocean or from the Mississippi River to the Pacific Ocean?
22. What country borders the United States on the north? on the south?
23. What river carved the Grand Canyon?
24. What is the deepest gorge (canyon) in the United States?
25. Which states are east of the Mississippi River—Ohio, Nebraska, Georgia, Maine, Wyoming?
26. Which states are west of the Mississippi—Utah, Indiana, Idaho, Illinois, Oregon?
27. Which state is usually the leading producer of petroleum (oil)?
28. What is the capital of your state? Is it the largest city?
29. What important document of the United States begins with the words "We the People of the United States, in Order to form a more perfect Union, . . ."?
30. What document begins, "When in the Course of human events, it becomes necessary for one people to dissolve the political bands which have connected them with another, . . ."?
31. What name did the sculptor of the Statue of Liberty give to the statue?
32. Where would you go to see the Liberty Bell?
33. What is the Continental Divide?
34. What is the Appalachian Trail?
35. What are the three branches of government in each of the states, as well as in the United States?
36. Which state has a unicameral legislature (a lawmaking body that has only one house, or chamber)?
37. What part of the Rocky Mountains is in Alaska?
38. Which state was built by the eruption of volcanoes?
39. Who is Uncle Sam?
40. Who were the Forty-niners?

Naming the States—a Memory Trick

Can you name the fifty states from memory? Most people probably cannot. Yet learning to name them is not hard to do if you think of them in alphabetical order. There are—

4 "A" STATES
Alabama
Alaska
Arizona
Arkansas

NO "B" STATES

3 "C" STATES
California
Colorado
Connecticut

1 "D" STATE
Delaware

NO "E" STATES

1 "F" STATE
Florida

1 "G" STATE
Georgia

1 "H" STATE
Hawaii

4 "I" STATES
Idaho
Illinois
Indiana
Iowa

NO "J" STATES

2 "K" STATES
Kansas
Kentucky

1 "L" STATE
Louisiana

8 "M" STATES
Maine
Maryland
Massachusetts
Michigan
Minnesota
Mississippi
Missouri
Montana

8 "N" STATES
(inc. 4 "New's"
and 2 "North's")
Nebraska
Nevada
New Hampshire
New Jersey
New Mexico
New York
North Carolina
North Dakota

3 "O" STATES
Ohio
Oklahoma
Oregon

1 "P" STATE
Pennsylvania

NO "Q" STATES

1 "R" STATE
Rhode Island

2 "S" STATES
South Carolina
South Dakota

2 "T" STATES
Tennessee
Texas

1 "U" STATE
Utah

2 "V" STATES
Vermont
Virginia

4 "W" STATES
Washington
West Virginia
Wisconsin
Wyoming

NO "X," "Y," OR
"Z" STATES

Can You Recognize These States?

The fifty states of the United States are like the members of a family. They are alike in some ways and different in others, as in size and shape. Can you recognize the states shown on the opposite page? Here are some clues:

COLORADO is an almost perfect rectangle. It is one of the few states with no boundaries formed by water.

MICHIGAN is made up of two parts. The lower part looks like a mitten.

OKLAHOMA is shaped like a cooking pot, with a long, straight handle pointing to the west.

IDAHO resembles the side view of a throne, or a chair with a high back.

LOUISIANA looks like a boot with a ragged toe.

TENNESSEE is long from east to west. It resembles a sled or an anvil.

CONNECTICUT, the third smallest state, is rectangular, except at the southwest corner.

WEST VIRGINIA has two parts called panhandles—one on the east and the other on the north.

CALIFORNIA, the third largest state, is shaped somewhat like a human arm, with a short upper arm and a long forearm bent toward the southeast.

MAINE looks somewhat like the head of a buffalo.

FLORIDA is long from north to south, with a panhandle pointing to the west.

MASSACHUSETTS ends in a ''hook'' in the east.

NEW JERSEY has about the same area as Massachusetts. But New Jersey is long and narrow, with zigzags on the west and the east.

ILLINOIS resembles an arrowhead, with part of one side broken off in a straight line.

DELAWARE, the second smallest state, has a northern boundary that is a perfect half-circle. In shape, Delaware looks somewhat like Idaho, but Idaho is about forty times larger.

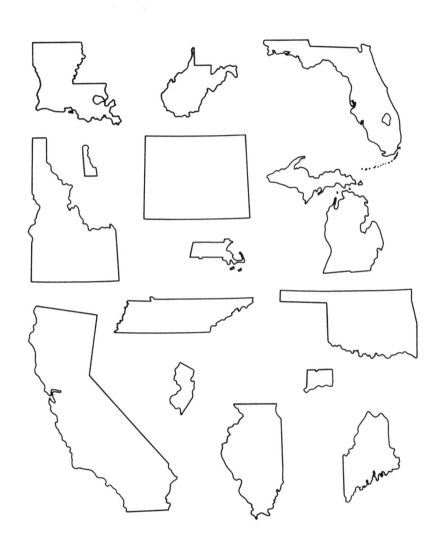

...and These?

Here are the rest of the states except Alaska and Hawaii. How many can you recognize from their shape and size? The capitals are shown as extra clues. To test yourself, try to match the numbers with the list of state names shown on each page. To see if you are right, check your answers against the map on pages 36 and 37.

ALABAMA
INDIANA
KANSAS
MINNESOTA
MONTANA
NEW YORK
NORTH CAROLINA
NORTH DAKOTA
OHIO
PENNSYLVANIA
RHODE ISLAND
SOUTH CAROLINA
TEXAS
VERMONT

ARIZONA
ARKANSAS
GEORGIA
IOWA
KENTUCKY
MARYLAND
MISSISSIPPI
MISSOURI
NEBRASKA
NEVADA
NEW HAMPSHIRE
NEW MEXICO
OREGON
SOUTH DAKOTA
UTAH
VIRGINIA
WASHINGTON
WISCONSIN
WYOMING

1 ★Phoenix

2 Little Rock ★

3 Cheyenne ★

4 ★Salem

5 Jackson ★

6 Des Moines ★

7 Salt Lake City ★

8 Frankfort ★

9 ★Atlanta

10 ★Olympia

11 ★Pierre

12 Madison ★

13 Richmond ★

14 Jefferson City ★

15 ★Carson City

16 Santa Fe ★

17 Annapolis ★

18 Concord ★

19 Lincoln ★

The Two Newest States

Alaska is so large that if a map of it were drawn to the same scale as the maps of the other states, it would need a whole page all for itself. For that reason it is not shown with the states on the preceding pages. This drawing shows a map of Alaska, with its many islands, placed over a map of the conterminous United States.* It helps you understand how big the mainland of Alaska is and how far Alaska extends from the north to the extreme southeast and from the southeast to the end of the island chain in the west.

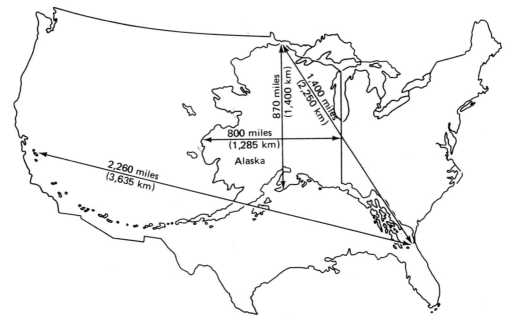

*The conterminous United States is the 48 states plus the District of Columbia, which made up the United States before Alaska gained statehood in 1959. Instead of "conterminous," you may sometimes see the word "coterminous" or "contiguous." All these have about the same meaning—"enclosed within the same boundary" or "touching one another." The conterminous United States plus Alaska is called the continental United States.

If the islands that make up the state of Hawaii were drawn to the same scale as the other states, they would be so small that you could not tell very much about them. Here is a map that shows the sizes and shapes of the eight main islands. In addition, the state includes numerous scattered islets, reefs, and shoals.

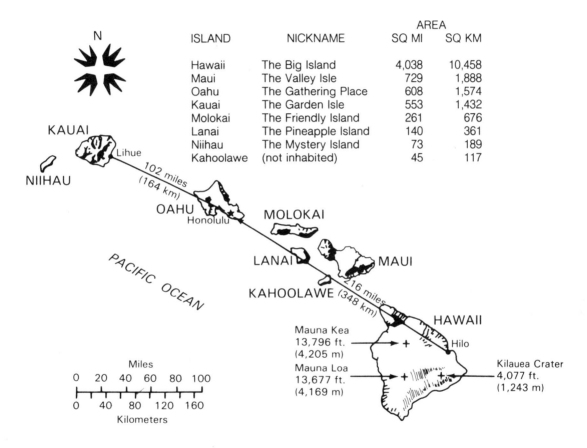

		AREA	
ISLAND	NICKNAME	SQ MI	SQ KM
Hawaii	The Big Island	4,038	10,458
Maui	The Valley Isle	729	1,888
Oahu	The Gathering Place	608	1,574
Kauai	The Garden Isle	553	1,432
Molokai	The Friendly Island	261	676
Lanai	The Pineapple Island	140	361
Niihau	The Mystery Island	73	189
Kahoolawe	(not inhabited)	45	117

KAUAI

Lihue

NIIHAU

102 miles
(164 km)

OAHU
Honolulu

MOLOKAI

PACIFIC OCEAN

LANAI

MAUI

KAHOOLAWE

216 miles
(348 km)

HAWAII

Mauna Kea
13,796 ft.
(4,205 m)

Hilo

Mauna Loa
13,677 ft.
(4,169 m)

Kilauea Crater
4,077 ft.
(1,243 m)

Miles
0 20 40 60 80 100

0 40 80 120 160
Kilometers

☆ President Thomas Jefferson bought the huge land area known as Louisiana from France for $15 million in 1803. This purchase, called the Louisiana Purchase, almost doubled the size of the United States at the time.

☆ The United States bought Alaska from Russia in 1867 for $7,200,000. The purchase was made by William H. Seward, U.S. Secretary of State under President Andrew Johnson.

☆ The kingdom of Hawaii was founded in 1810 by a warrior chief who became King Kamehameha I. The kingdom lasted until 1893, when a republic was established. The legislature of the republic asked the United States to annex (join) the islands to the United States. They were annexed as a territory in 1898.

How the United States Began—and How It Grew

The United States of America—also called the United States, the U.S.A., or sometimes "the States"—is a nation, or country, of the world. It takes its name from the fact that it is made up of states that are joined together, or united, by the Constitution to form one nation.

It began as thirteen colonies of England, spread out along the central Atlantic coast of North America. But the colonies did not come into being all at once. In fact, about 125 years passed between the founding of Virginia, the first colony, in 1607 and the founding of Georgia, the thirteenth, in 1733. More time passed—forty-three years—until the colonies joined together, rebelled against England, and declared on July 4, 1776, "That these United Colonies are, and of Right ought to be, Free and Independent States." This declaration (statement) was made in the now-famous document (official writing, or paper) called the Declaration of Independence.

To gain freedom, the colonies fought the War of Independence, also called the Revolutionary War or the American Revolution. The treaty of peace ending the war (called the Peace of Paris) was signed in Paris on September 3, 1783. By this treaty England gave up its claim to the thirteen colonies, as well as to all land east of the Mississippi River from Canada to Florida.

The map on the opposite page shows when and how the United States added the land from which the other states were formed.

The map on the opposite page is from the *Statistical Abstract of the United States*, published each year by the Bureau of the Census, U.S. Department of Commerce, Washington, D.C.

National Documents and Symbols

THE DECLARATION OF INDEPENDENCE

The Declaration of Independence begins:

When in the Course of human events, it becomes necessary for one people to dissolve the political bands which have connected them with another, and to assume among the powers of the earth, the separate and equal station to which the Laws of Nature and of Nature's God entitle them, a decent respect to the opinions of mankind requires that they should declare the causes which impel them to the separation. . . .

THE LIBERTY BELL

The Liberty Bell, with its famous crack, stands in a special pavilion in Independence National Historical Park in Philadelphia. The Pennsylvania Assembly ordered the bell from London, but it was cracked by a stroke of its clapper soon after it arrived in 1752. It was recast in Philadelphia and was hung in the State House (later called Independence Hall) in 1753. The bell was rung after the Continental Congress, meeting in the State House, had adopted the Declaration of Independence and on many other important occasions until it cracked again in 1835. It sounded for the last time on George Washington's birthday in 1846. It was then taken down and kept in the State House until it was moved to its present location on January 1, 1976, the beginning of the nation's bicentennial year.

The Liberty Bell weighs 2,080 pounds (943 kg) and is 3 feet (0.9 m) high and 12 feet (3.7 m) in circumference around the bottom. Inscribed on the bell is a quotation from the Bible (Leviticus 25:10): "Proclaim liberty throughout all the land unto all the inhabitants thereof."

THE CONSTITUTION

We the People of the United States, in order to form a more perfect Union, insure domestic Tranquility, provide for the common defence, promote the general Welfare, and secure the Blessings of Liberty to ourselves and our Posterity, do ordain and establish this Constitution for the United States of America.

This is the preamble (introduction) to the Constitution:

> *We the People of the United States, in Order to form a more perfect Union, establish Justice, insure domestic Tranquility, provide for the common defence, promote the general Welfare, and secure the Blessings of Liberty to ourselves and our Posterity, do ordain and establish this Constitution for the United States of America.*

THE STATUE OF LIBERTY

The Statue of Liberty, a gift of the people of France to the United States, stands on Liberty Island in New York Harbor. It was planned to celebrate the 100th anniversary, in 1876, of the Declaration of Independence, as well as the friendship between the two countries that began when France helped the thirteen colonies win independence.

The statue was created by the sculptor Frédéric Auguste Bartholdi, using hammered copper sheets mounted on an iron framework. He named it Liberty Enlightening the World. The gigantic statue was not finished until 1884. It was then taken apart and shipped to New York. After the foundation and pedestal were completed, it was put back together and was dedicated in 1886.

By the early 1980s the statue had deteriorated badly. Many people, including expert workers from France, helped restore it in time for a great celebration of its 100th birthday, held on July 4, 1986.

The statue, Liberty Island, and nearby Ellis Island, where many immigrants entered the United States, make up the Statue of Liberty National Monument, managed by the National Park Service.

The statue weighs 225 tons (205 metric tons). It is 151 feet (46 m) high to the top of the torch. With the pedestal and foundation, it towers 305 feet (93 m) above the harbor.

UNCLE SAM

Uncle Sam is a popular nickname and symbol of the United States government. The symbol usually appears as a figure with white hair and chin whiskers, wearing a long coat, striped trousers, and a top hat with stars or stars and stripes. The nickname was first used during the War of 1812. Most stories say it came from the name of Samuel Wilson, the owner of a meat-packing plant in Troy, New York, who served as a government inspector of meat for the army during the war. One day, when visitors to Wilson's plant asked what the markings on barrels of inspected meat stood for, a worker explained some of them—and then jokingly added that the letters "U.S." (the abbreviation of "United States") stood for "Uncle Sam" Wilson. Years later, in 1961, Congress passed a resolution recognizing "Uncle Sam" Wilson as the person for whom the symbol was named.

A now-famous image of Uncle Sam appeared on a World War I Army recruiting poster by the illustrator James Montgomery Flagg. It shows Uncle Sam pointing a finger and saying, "I Want You."

THE EAGLE AND THE GREAT SEAL

The bald eagle became a national emblem in 1782, when it was selected as the main feature in the design of the Great Seal of the United States. The seal is the "signature" of the United States, used on all official documents. The eagle holds in its claws an olive branch and arrows, standing for peace and strength. In its beak it holds a streamer bearing a motto in Latin, *E pluribus unum* (Out of many [colonies], one [nation]).

The back of the seal also has a design, but it is never used on documents. (Both designs appear on the one-dollar bill.) The back design shows an unfinished pyramid, standing for the United States, with thirteen rows of stones (the thirteen colonies) watched over by an eye (the all-seeing Eye of God). The date 1776 in Roman numerals appears at the base of the pyramid. There are two Latin mottoes, *Annuit coeptis* (He [God] has smiled on our undertakings) and *Novus ordo seclorum* (A new order of the ages).

FLAG: The Stars and Stripes
NATIONAL ANTHEM: "The Star-Spangled Banner," by Francis Scott Key (adopted by Congress in 1931)
MOTTO: In God We Trust (adopted in 1956)
FLORAL EMBLEM: The rose (adopted in 1986)

The Birthdays of the States

The date of the Declaration of Independence—July 4, 1776—is the official "birthday" of the United States. Each of the original thirteen states might call July 4, 1776, its birthday, too.

Why, then, is Delaware sometimes called the first state, Pennsylvania the second, and so on?

To understand why, we need to know certain facts about the Constitution of the United States.

After the War of Independence, the thirteen states were united under a form of government called the Articles of Confederation. But they soon realized that they needed a new and stronger form of national government.

In May 1787 the states sent delegates, or representatives, to a meeting in Philadelphia called the Constitutional Convention. The delegates prepared a new form of government, which they detailed in the Constitution of the United States of America. They finished their work on September 17, 1787. Then a copy of the Constitution was sent to each of the thirteen states.

The people in each state chose delegates to study the Constitution and decide whether the state would ratify (approve) it. It was agreed that the Constitution would become the official form of government when nine of the thirteen states had voted to approve it. Delaware was the first to do so, and New Hampshire the ninth.

The Constitution provided that new states might be admitted by the Congress of the United States. Before they gained statehood, most of the other thirty-seven states passed through a stage when they were known as territories of the United States. The territories were organized by Congress, and the chief officers were appointed by the president and the U.S. Senate. When the people in a territory felt that they were ready to form a state government, they would elect delegates to prepare a state constitution. Then they would vote to decide whether they would accept the constitution and ask to be admitted to the Union.

The signing of the U.S. Constitution
in 1787 by a majority of delegates to
the Constitutional Convention

The following list shows the order in which the thirteen states ratified the Constitution:

1st	DELAWARE	December 7, 1787
2nd	PENNSYLVANIA	December 12, 1787
3rd	NEW JERSEY	December 18, 1787
4th	GEORGIA	January 2, 1788
5th	CONNECTICUT	January 9, 1788
6th	MASSACHUSETTS	February 6, 1788
7th	MARYLAND	April 28, 1788
8th	SOUTH CAROLINA	May 23, 1788
9th	NEW HAMPSHIRE	June 21, 1788
10th	VIRGINIA	June 25, 1788
11th	NEW YORK	July 26, 1788
12th	NORTH CAROLINA	November 21, 1789
13th	RHODE ISLAND	May 29, 1790

The list on page 22 shows when the other states were organized as separate territories, when they were admitted to the Union (their official "birthdays"), and the order in which they were admitted. The notes that follow the list explain how states that were not organized as separate territories achieved statehood.

The official names of most of the states include the words "State of," as in State of Alabama, State of Alaska. But four of the states call themselves commonwealths instead of states. ("Commonwealth," as used in this sense, means the same as "state.") Their official names are Commonwealth of Kentucky, Commonwealth of Massachusetts, Commonwealth of Pennsylvania, and Commonwealth of Virginia.

STATE	ORGANIZED AS A TERRITORY	ADMITTED TO THE UNION	ORDER OF ADMISSION
VERMONT		March 4, 1791	14th
KENTUCKY		June 1, 1792	15th
TENNESSEE		June 1, 1796	16th
OHIO		March 1, 1803	17th
LOUISIANA	1804	April 30, 1812	18th
INDIANA	1800	December 11, 1816	19th
MISSISSIPPI	1798	December 10, 1817	20th
ILLINOIS	1809	December 3, 1818	21st
ALABAMA	1817	December 14, 1819	22nd
MAINE		March 15, 1820	23rd
MISSOURI	1812	August 10, 1821	24th
ARKANSAS	1819	June 15, 1836	25th
MICHIGAN	1805	January 26, 1837	26th
FLORIDA	1822	March 3, 1845	27th
TEXAS		December 29, 1845	28th
IOWA	1838	December 28, 1846	29th
WISCONSIN	1836	May 29, 1848	30th
CALIFORNIA		September 9, 1850	31st
MINNESOTA	1849	May 11, 1858	32nd
OREGON	1848	February 14, 1859	33rd
KANSAS	1854	January 29, 1861	34th
WEST VIRGINIA		June 20, 1863	35th
NEVADA	1861	October 31, 1864	36th
NEBRASKA	1854	March 1, 1867	37th
COLORADO	1861	August 1, 1876	38th
NORTH DAKOTA	1861	November 2, 1889	39th*
SOUTH DAKOTA	1861	November 2, 1889	40th*
MONTANA	1864	November 8, 1889	41st
WASHINGTON	1853	November 11, 1889	42nd
IDAHO	1863	July 3, 1890	43rd
WYOMING	1868	July 10, 1890	44th
UTAH	1850	January 4, 1896	45th
OKLAHOMA	1890	November 16, 1907	46th
NEW MEXICO	1850	January 6, 1912	47th
ARIZONA	1863	February 14, 1912	48th
ALASKA	1912	January 3, 1959	49th
HAWAII	1900	August 21, 1959	50th

*When the official papers admitting North Dakota and South Dakota were signed, the names of the states were covered so that no one would know which one was admitted first. But the two states agreed that North Dakota would be the 39th state, and South Dakota, the 40th.

☆ Vermont was formed from lands claimed by both New Hampshire and New York. The dispute continued until 1777, when Vermont declared itself a free and independent republic. Finally the claims were settled, and Vermont became the fourteenth state.

☆ Kentucky was part of Virginia until admitted as a state.

☆ Before Tennessee became a state, it was first part of western North Carolina and then part of a large area known as the Territory South of the River Ohio.

☆ Before Ohio became a state, it was part of a large area known as the Territory Northwest of the River Ohio.

☆ Maine was part of Massachusetts until its admission to the Union as a separate state.

☆ Texas was an independent country, known as the Republic of Texas, from 1836 until it was admitted as a state of the United States.

☆ California prepared a constitution and used it to set up a government almost a year before it was admitted to the Union.

☆ West Virginia was part of Virginia until admitted as a state.

What Is the District of Columbia?

The initials "D.C." in the name of the national capital, Washington, D.C., stand for "District of Columbia." The district was named for Christopher Columbus. It is situated on the Potomac River, on land that once was part of the State of Maryland. Because the city of Washington covers the whole area, the names "Washington, D.C." and "District of Columbia" actually have the same meaning. The city was named for George Washington.

At first the district included 100 square miles (about 260 sq km) given to the federal government by Maryland and Virginia in 1791. But Virginia's part was returned in 1846. The area is now 69 square miles (178 sq km).

Washington, D.C., is a federal district (an area set apart as the seat of the United States government), not a state or a part of any state. Actually, it is two cities in one. It is the federal city, with government buildings, parks, and monuments. It is also, like any other city, the home of a large number of people.

For more than one hundred years, the Congress of the United States appointed officials to govern the city. But since 1974, Washington, D.C., has had self-government. The people elect a mayor, who is the chief executive officer, and a thirteen-member council, which makes the laws. The people also have the right to vote for president and vice-president, as well as the right to elect a delegate to the U.S. House of Representatives. The delegate takes part in the work of the House but does not have a vote.

More than half of the people work in offices of the federal government. Many others have jobs in the tourist industry.

How Were the States Named?

About half of the states have names of Indian origin. Most of the others were named for persons or places.

ALABAMA: Probably from Indian words *alba ayamule*, meaning "I make a clearing."

ALASKA: From the Aleut word *alakshak*, meaning "peninsula."

ARIZONA: Probably from the Indian word *arizonac*, meaning "few springs" or "small springs."

ARKANSAS: From Indians, the Quapaws, meaning "downstream people"; they were called "Arkansas" by French explorers.

CALIFORNIA: Probably from the name of an imaginary island in a sixteenth-century Spanish novel. Explorers gave the name to the peninsula because they thought it resembled the island called California in the novel.

COLORADO: From the Spanish word *colorado*, meaning "red"; the name was first given to the Colorado River by Spanish explorers, to whom the waters looked reddish.

CONNECTICUT: Probably from the Indian words *quinnitukq-ut*, meaning "at the long tidal river." The name was first given to the Connecticut River, which is a tidal river, or river that flows into an ocean and is affected by the tides.

DELAWARE: From the Delaware River, named in honor of Lord Delaware (the title of Thomas West, also known as Baron De La Warr), one of the first governors of Virginia.

FLORIDA: From the Spanish words *Pascua florida*, meaning "flowery Easter." The name was chosen by the Spanish explorer Ponce de Leon because of the flowery appearance of the land and his discovery of it during the Easter season.

GEORGIA: For King George II of England.

HAWAII: Possibly from *Havaiki*, the legendary homeland of Polynesians who settled on the Hawaiian Islands.

IDAHO: Probably of Indian origin, although scholars have been unable to trace it in Indian languages.

ILLINOIS: From words in Indian languages meaning "man"; the French changed the words to Illinois.

INDIANA: From the word *Indian* plus the *-a* ending used in many geographical names.

IOWA: From the Indian word *Ayuhwa*, meaning "sleepy ones."

KANSAS: From *Kansa*, or *Kansas*, the name of a tribe of Indians who once lived in the area.

KENTUCKY: Probably related to the Indian word *kenta*, meaning "level" or "prairie," referring to the level land in the south central part of the state.

LOUISIANA: For Louis XIV, King of France.

MAINE: Probably named by French explorers in the 1500s for Maine, an old region of France.

MARYLAND: Named *Terra Mariae* (Latin words meaning "Land of Maria") by King Charles I of England for his wife, Queen Henrietta Maria.

MASSACHUSETTS: From Massachusetts Bay, which was named for the Massachusetts Indians, who lived around the Blue Hills near Boston; the name is made up of Indian words meaning "about the big hill."

MICHIGAN: From Lake Michigan, which takes its name from Indian words meaning "large lake."

MINNESOTA: From the Minnesota River, named from the Indian word *minisota*, meaning "white water."

MISSISSIPPI: From the Mississippi River, named from Indian words *misi*, meaning "big," and *sipi*, "river."

MISSOURI: From the Missouri River, named for an Indian people, the Missouri, whose name means "owners of big canoes."

MONTANA: From the Latin word *montana*, meaning "mountainous regions."

NEBRASKA: From Indian words used as the early name of the Platte River. Later, the river received its present name and the state received the Indian name.

NEVADA: Named for the Sierra Nevada, a mountain range on the western border of the state. *Sierra* is Spanish for "mountain range," and *nevada* means "snow-covered."

NEW HAMPSHIRE: From the county of Hampshire in England.

NEW JERSEY: From Jersey, an island off the coast of England.

NEW MEXICO: Named for the country of Mexico.

NEW YORK: For James, Duke of York and Albany, who received the land from his brother, King Charles II of England.

NORTH CAROLINA: From *Carolus*, the Latin form of Charles, in honor of King Charles I of England. (See South Carolina.)

NORTH DAKOTA: From the Dakota Indians; the name means "allies."

OHIO: From the Ohio River, which perhaps was named from an Indian word, *oheo*, meaning "beautiful."

OKLAHOMA: From Indian words *okla humma*, or *okla homma*, meaning "red people."

OREGON: From Oregon River, an early name of the Columbia River.

PENNSYLVANIA: For Sir William Penn, father of William Penn, the founder of Pennsylvania. The last part of the name (-*sylvania*) comes from the Latin word for "wood" or "forest."

RHODE ISLAND: The earliest settlements were called "plantations." The first was named Providence by its founder, Roger Williams, "in commemoration of God's merciful providence." Later, the settlements of Portsmouth and Newport were incorporated with Providence under the name Providence Plantations. The largest island in Narragansett Bay, Aquidneck, was renamed Rhode Island, possibly after the Isle of Rhodes in the Aegean Sea. In 1663 the settlements adopted what is now the official name of the state—Rhode Island and Providence Plantations. In this way, Rhode Island, the smallest state—nicknamed Little Rhody—came to have the longest name.

SOUTH CAROLINA: Same as North Carolina; the two Carolinas began as a single colony, which later was divided into a northern and a southern part.

SOUTH DAKOTA: Same as North Dakota; the Dakotas began as the territory of Dakota, which was divided into two parts.

TENNESSEE: From the Tennessee River, which was named for an Indian village called Tanasi.

TEXAS: From *techas*, an Indian word meaning "allies" or "friends."

UTAH: From Yuta, the Ute Indians' name for themselves.

VERMONT: From French words meaning "green mountains."

VIRGINIA: Named after Queen Elizabeth I of England, who was known as the Virgin Queen because she was unmarried.

WASHINGTON: Named for George Washington, the first president of the United States.

WEST VIRGINIA: So named because it originally was the western part of Virginia.

WISCONSIN: Probably from the Indian word *wishkonsing*, meaning "place of the beaver."

WYOMING: From Indian words meaning "on the great plain." The name was first given to the Wyoming Valley in eastern Pennsylvania.

How Were the Capitals Named?

Almost half of the state capitals were named in honor of persons. The others were named in various ways.

Two were named for Christopher Columbus:

COLUMBUS, Ohio, and COLUMBIA, South Carolina.

Four have names honoring presidents of the United States:

JACKSON, Mississippi, for Andrew Jackson.
JEFFERSON CITY, Missouri, for Thomas Jefferson.
LINCOLN, Nebraska, for Abraham Lincoln.
MADISON, Wisconsin, for James Madison.

Seventeen were named for other persons:

MONTGOMERY, Alabama: For General Richard Montgomery, a hero of the Revolutionary War.
JUNEAU, Alaska: For Joe Juneau, a prospector who found gold in the area in 1880.
DENVER, Colorado: For James William Denver, governor in 1858 of Kansas Territory, which included Colorado.
FRANKFORT, Kentucky: First called Frank's Ford for a pioneer, Stephen Frank, who was killed by Indians at a ford (river crossing) in the Kentucky River.
AUGUSTA, Maine: Probably for Augusta Dearborn, daughter of Henry Dearborn, a Revolutionary War general.
ANNAPOLIS, Maryland: For Queen Anne of England. (The ending -polis is the Greek word for "city.")
SAINT PAUL, Minnesota: For Saint Paul, to whom in 1841 Father Lucien Galtier dedicated a log church, around which a settlement, also called Saint Paul, grew.
CARSON CITY, Nevada: For Christopher (Kit) Carson, Indian scout and frontiersman.
TRENTON, New Jersey: For William Trent, a Philadelphia businessman who laid out the town.
ALBANY, New York: For James, Duke of York and Albany (later King James II of England).
RALEIGH, North Carolina: For Sir Walter Raleigh, an English navigator.
BISMARCK, North Dakota: For the German leader Bismarck.

HARRISBURG, Pennsylvania: For John Harris, who established a trading post at the site.

PIERRE, South Dakota: For Pierre Chouteau, a member of the family who helped to found St. Louis, Missouri, and later made a fortune trading with the Indians.

NASHVILLE, Tennessee: For Francis Nash, a Revolutionary War general.

AUSTIN, Texas: For Stephen F. Austin, a leader in Texas's struggle for independence from Mexico.

CHARLESTON, West Virginia: For Charles Clendenin; named by his son Colonel George Clendenin, a Revolutionary War soldier and owner of the land on which the settlement was built.

Three were named for other cities or towns:

LANSING, Michigan: For Lansing, a village in New York.

HELENA, Montana: For Helena, Minnesota.

MONTPELIER, Vermont: Probably for Montpellier, France.

Two capitals were named for their states:

INDIANAPOLIS, Indiana, and OKLAHOMA CITY, Oklahoma.

Four are namesakes of cities or towns in England:

HARTFORD, Connecticut; DOVER, Delaware; BOSTON, Massachusetts; and RICHMOND, Virginia.

Five capitals take their names from physical features:

LITTLE ROCK, Arkansas: From a rocky formation on the bank of the Arkansas River.

HONOLULU, Hawaii: The name is Hawaiian for "sheltered bay."

SPRINGFIELD, Illinois: Probably from a creek called Spring Creek on land where the settlement was built.

SALT LAKE CITY, Utah: From Great Salt Lake.

OLYMPIA, Washington: From the Olympic Mountains.

Eight capitals have Indian, French, or Spanish names:

SACRAMENTO, California: From *Sacramento*, a Spanish word meaning "the Blessed Sacrament."

TALLAHASSEE, Florida: From an Indian word meaning "old field" or "old town."

BOISE, Idaho: Named by French Canadians, who, after journeying through treeless country, are said to have exclaimed *"Les bois!"* ("The woods!" or "The trees!") when they saw trees in the vicinity of the present city.

DES MOINES, Iowa: From the Des Moines River, which was probably named for an Indian tribe called Moingouena. French explorers called the river Rivière des Moingouenas, and then Rivière des Moings.

TOPEKA, Kansas: From an Indian word meaning "a good place to dig potatoes, or roots."

BATON ROUGE, Louisiana: From a red post or stick (*baton rouge*, in French) that was used to mark the boundary between the hunting grounds of two Indian tribes.

SANTA FE, New Mexico: A shortened form of the original Spanish name *La Villa Real de la Santa Fe de San Francisco de Asis* ("The Royal City of the Holy Faith of Saint Francis of Assisi").

CHEYENNE, Wyoming: For the Cheyenne Indians.

Three capitals were named for ideas:

CONCORD, New Hampshire: For the idea of concord (meaning "state of agreement, or harmony").

SALEM, Oregon: From the Hebrew word *shalom* (which means "well-being" or "peace").

PROVIDENCE, Rhode Island: Named in commemoration of "God's merciful providence" ("providence" meaning "divine guidance or care").

The rest got their names in these ways:

PHOENIX, Arizona: From the mythical bird the phoenix. Early settlers founded the city in the 1860s on lands where the prehistoric Hohokam Indians had built irrigation canals to water their crops. The settlers rebuilt some of the canals and predicted that a new city would arise "phoenixlike" where ancient Indian pueblos once stood. (According to mythology, the phoenix caused itself to be destroyed by fire and then arose from its ashes more beautiful and youthful than ever before.)

ATLANTA, Georgia: From the word "Atlantic" in the name of the Western and Atlantic Railroad; the city was the southeastern terminus of the railroad.

How Are the States Governed?

All fifty states have similar forms of government. Each has a constitution, much like the Constitution of the United States, which divides the powers of government among three branches.

The legislative branch legislates (makes the laws).

The executive branch executes (carries out) the laws.

The judicial branch, which is made up of a system of courts, judges questions about the laws.

The head of the executive branch of the national government is the president. The head in each state is the governor.

The legislative branch of the national government is the Congress of the United States. It is made up of two bodies, or chambers, called the Senate and the House of Representatives. In all of the states except one (Nebraska), the legislative branch also is made up of two bodies.

All of the states call this branch by the general name "legislature." Twenty-seven use "Legislature" as the official name, nineteen use "General Assembly," two use "Legislative Assembly," and two use "General Court."

Nebraska has a unicameral legislature—that is, a legislature of only one body, or chamber. All of the other states, like the national government, have bicameral lawmaking bodies. (The prefix *uni-* means "one," and the prefix *bi-* means "two.") All of the states call one body the Senate, and most of them call the other body the House of Representatives.

Each state, like the nation, has a capital and a capitol. These words sometimes are confused, but they should not be.

Capital (spelled with *-tal* as the last syllable) means "city that is the seat of government."

Capitol (spelled with *-tol* as the last syllable) means "the building where the legislative branch of government meets."

In most states—but not all—the official name of the capitol is either "State Capitol" or "State House." Most of the capitols are stately buildings with domes, somewhat like the Capitol of the United States in the national capital, Washington, D.C.

A Trip Across the States

Where does the United States rank in size (area) among countries of the world? It is fourth, behind the Soviet Union, Canada, and China. Forty-eight of the fifty states lie in the middle of the North American continent. They stretch from the Atlantic Ocean on the east to the Pacific Ocean on the west, a distance of nearly 3,000 miles (4,800 km). The north-south distance—from the Canadian border to Mexico and the Gulf of Mexico—is about half as great. With Alaska and Hawaii, the United States extends far into the Pacific. Hawaii is about 2,400 miles (3,900 km) from the coast of California.

How can we describe the huge land area of the forty-eight states? The map on pages 36 and 37 shows the main features. There are two great mountain systems—the Appalachians in the east and the Rocky Mountains in the west—with a broad lowland stretching out between them. There are many other landforms besides these. A low coastal plain extends along the Atlantic Ocean and the Gulf of Mexico. And there is another main mountain rib west of the Rockies. It is made up of the Sierra Nevada and the Cascade Range.

To have a closer look at the land, let us board a low-flying plane on the Atlantic coast near Richmond, Virginia, and fly westward across the midsection of the country. We shall have a magical wide-angle viewer, so we can see far and wide.

As we take off over the coastal plain, we look to the north. The view in that direction helps us understand the meaning of the word "megalopolis"—a very large urban, or city, area. We see a seemingly endless city spread out along the coast. In this crowded megalopolis, we pick out Washington, D.C., Baltimore, Philadelphia, New York, and Boston.

South of Richmond, the view is quite different. We see cities, of course. But beaches, swamps, and sandy offshore islands catch our eye—all the way to the southern tip of Florida and then along the coast of the Gulf of Mexico.

When we turn to the scene ahead, we are nearing the Appalachians. Quickly we look to the northeast to see where this mountain system begins (in Maine) and then to the southwest to see where it ends (in Alabama). We wish we could explore the many forested ranges, follow the rushing rivers, and stand by the sparkling lakes and waterfalls. We could do this if we packed our knapsacks someday and set out along the Appalachian Trail—a footpath for hikers that the National Park Service has marked out from one end of the Appalachians to the other. Directly below, we see where coal is dug from these mountains, especially in West Virginia and Kentucky. And we look for Cumberland Gap, the pass through the mountains where, in 1775, Daniel Boone helped carve out a road that pioneers could follow westward. The Appalachians are not high. But before that time, they served as a wall that kept settlers on the eastern side of the mountains.

Looking to the north, we see the Ohio River, flowing westward. North of the river, beginning in the state of Ohio, is the Central Lowland, which stretches as far as Kansas. This is prairie country. Once it was a vast sea of grass that grew taller than the pioneers' wagon wheels. Today it is a land where tall corn grows, along with many other crops. We see big cities, too, especially along the Great Lakes. Chicago, at the southern tip of Lake Michigan, is the giant among them.

South of Ohio and the Appalachians are the states that once made up the cotton-growing South. Today the states in that region grow many crops besides cotton. They are part of what is now called the Sun Belt. It extends all the way across the country, from the Carolinas and Florida to California.

Looking ahead again, we see a great river—the Mississippi—winding southward to the Gulf of Mexico. Directly below, the Ohio flows into the Mississippi. We look quickly to the north and then to the south to see where two rivers flowing from the west—the Missouri and the Arkansas—join the Mississippi in this area. As we cross the state of Missouri, we look southward for a glimpse of the Ozark Mountains and northward for a view of Iowa's rich farmlands and Minnesota's and Wisconsin's beautiful lakes and forests.

The scene below changes quickly. The land is flat and almost treeless. This is the Great Plains, extending from the Dakotas to Texas. Once it was a grassland where buffalo roamed. Now it is a land of wheat and cattle. But farmers there must farm in ways that conserve the soil. In the 1930s this region was called the Dust Bowl. The nat-

The United States

Red River of

MINNESOTA
Duluth
Sault Ste. Marie
Lake Superior
Quebec
MAINE
Augusta
VT.
Montreal
Ottawa
Montpelier
N.H.
Portland
Concord
MICHIGAN
St. Paul
WISCONSIN
Minneapolis
Lake Michigan
Lake Huron
MASS.
Boston
Madison
Grand Rapids
Flint
Toronto
Lake Ontario
Albany
Hartford
Providence
R.I.
Milwaukee
Lansing
Buffalo
NEW YORK
HIGHLANDS
CONN.
New York
Sioux City
IOWA
Davenport
Chicago
Detroit
Lake Erie
N.J.
Trenton
Des Moines
Gary
Cleveland
PENNSYLVANIA
Pittsburgh
Philadelphia
Peoria
OHIO
Harrisburg
Baltimore
Dover
DEL.
ILLINOIS
INDIANA
Columbus
Washington
Annapolis
MD.
Kansas City
Springfield
Indianapolis
Cincinnati
WEST
D.C.
ncoln
Jefferson City
VIRGINIA
peka
St. Louis
Ohio River
Frankfort
Charleston
Richmond
ansas City
Kansas City
Lexington
VIRGINIA
Norfolk
Louisville
Wichita
MISSOURI
KENTUCKY
NORTH
Mt. Mitchell
6,684 ft.
Raleigh
Tulsa
Nashville
(2,039 m)
CAROLINA
klahoma City
ARKANSAS
TENNESSEE
Charlotte
AHOMA
Ft. Smith
Memphis
Tennessee R.
SOUTH
Columbia
River
Little Rock
CAROLINA
Charleston
Birmingham
Atlanta
Dallas
ALABAMA
GEORGIA
Savannah
Shreveport
Jackson
t Worth
LOUISIANA
Montgomery
ustin
Baton Rouge
Mobile
Tallahassee
Jacksonville
Houston
New Orleans
Galveston
Cape Canaveral
FLORIDA
Tampa
GULF OF MEXICO
Miami
STRAITS OF FLORIDA
TROPIC OF CANCER
Havana
CUBA
ATLANTIC

0   200   400   600   800 Miles
0 200 400 600 800 1000 1200 km

95°W   90°W   85°W   80°W   75°W

ural grasses that held the soil together had been plowed up, and the soil was loose and crumbly. A long period of drought came, and wind blew tons of topsoil away. Many families left their ruined farms.

The land in eastern Colorado is flat, but we see the Rocky Mountains looming ahead. They extend from New Mexico to the Canadian border, on through Canada, and on westward into Alaska north of the Arctic Circle. There they are called the Brooks Range. The highest peaks and ridges of the Rockies form an imaginary line called the Continental Divide. Rivers that begin west of that line flow westward to the Pacific, and those that begin to the east flow eastward.

To the north and south, we see a maze of peaks and gorges. Some parts are forested, dotted with lakes and cut by rushing rivers. Others seem dry and bare. Those mountains have valuable deposits of gold, silver, copper, coal, and other minerals. We see famous old mining towns and well-known ski resorts of today. We see why the Rockies are a year-round vacationland.

As we speed westward, we look down on a region of high plateaus and short, rugged mountain ranges separated by desert basins. The plateaus are cut by deep gorges. We have been keeping an eye on the Colorado River. And now, to the south, we see the work that it has done in carving the incredible Grand Canyon in northern Arizona. In this dry country we look for another famous spot, the deep desert valley in eastern California called Death Valley.

Again, mountains come into view. These are the Sierra Nevadas. To the south is Mount Whitney, the highest point in the United States outside Alaska. Strangely enough, Mount Whitney is quite close to Death Valley, the lowest point in the country. The Sierras remind us of gold because it was gold in the Sierras that brought a great rush of settlers, called Forty-niners, to California in 1849. We look to the north for a view of the Cascade Range in Oregon and Washington. The peaks there were built by volcanoes. One of these, Mount St. Helens in Washington, erupted suddenly and violently in May 1980. Many peaks in the Aleutian Range in Alaska are active volcanoes, and all of the islands of Hawaii are the tops of volcanic mountains.

Now we pass over the fertile Central Valley of California. There and in the irrigated Imperial Valley to the south, people are busy harvesting huge quantities of fruits, vegetables, and other foods that will find their way to dinner tables all over the country. Ahead is San Francisco, on San Francisco Bay. There our journey ends.

From Mather Point Overlook, visitors can see
the spectacular Grand Canyon stretching out before them.

*Hells Canyon of the Snake River, on the Idaho-Oregon
border, is one of the world's deepest gorges.*

Highests, Lowests, Biggests, Mosts

Here are some interesting facts about features of the fifty states:

HIGHEST POINT: Mount McKinley, Alaska—20,320 feet (6,198 m) above sea level.

LOWEST POINT: Death Valley, California—282 feet (86 m) below sea level.

NORTHERNMOST POINT: Point Barrow, Alaska.

SOUTHERNMOST POINT: Ka Lae (South Cape), island of Hawaii (State of Hawaii).

EASTERNMOST POINT: West Quoddy Head, Maine.

WESTERNMOST POINT: Cape Wrangell, Attu Island (one of the Aleutian Islands), Alaska.

DEEPEST GORGE: Hells Canyon of the Snake River, on the Idaho-Oregon border—7,900 feet (2,400 m).

HIGHEST TEMPERATURE EVER RECORDED: 134°Fahrenheit (56.7°Celsius), Death Valley, California.

LOWEST TEMPERATURE EVER RECORDED: −79.8°Fahrenheit (−62.1°Celsius), Prospect Creek Camp, Alaska.

WETTEST PLACE: Mount Waialeale, on the island of Kauai (State of Hawaii)—average yearly rainfall, 460 inches (11,680 mm).

STRONGEST SURFACE WIND EVER RECORDED: 231 miles (372 km) per hour, Mount Washington, New Hampshire.

LONGEST RIVER: Missouri-Mississippi system—3,710 miles (5,970 km).

HIGHEST WATERFALLS: Yosemite Falls, in Yosemite National Park, California—2,425 feet (740 m) in three stages.

BIGGEST TREE: The General Sherman, a giant sequoia in Sequoia National Park, California—275 feet (84 m) tall and 83 feet (25 m) in girth.

TALLEST TREE: a coast redwood in Humboldt Redwoods State Park, California—362 feet (110 m).

OLDEST LIVING TREES: Bristlecone pines, chiefly in California, some of which are thought to be more than 4,600 years old.

STATES SURROUNDED BY THE MOST OTHER STATES: Missouri and Tennessee, each surrounded by eight other states.

A PLACE WHERE YOU COULD STAND IN FOUR STATES ALL AT ONCE: The "Four Corners" of Utah, Colorado, New Mexico, and Arizona—the only place where the corners of four states touch.

The Size of the States—Area and Population

The list below ranks the states by area. You can use the list to compare them. For example, Alaska is how many times larger than Rhode Island? How many times larger than Texas? Which states are of medium size? Which states have about the same area?

RANK		AREA*	
		SQ MI	SQ KM
1	ALASKA	591,004	1,530,700
2	TEXAS	266,807	691,030
3	CALIFORNIA	158,706	411,049
4	MONTANA	147,046	380,848
5	NEW MEXICO	121,593	314,925
6	ARIZONA	114,000	295,260
7	NEVADA	110,561	286,352
8	COLORADO	104,091	269,595
9	WYOMING	97,809	253,326
10	OREGON	97,073	251,419
11	UTAH	84,899	219,889
12	MINNESOTA	84,402	218,601
13	IDAHO	83,564	216,432
14	KANSAS	82,277	213,098
15	NEBRASKA	77,355	200,350
16	SOUTH DAKOTA	77,116	199,730
17	NORTH DAKOTA	70,702	183,119
18	OKLAHOMA	69,956	181,186
19	MISSOURI	69,697	180,516
20	WASHINGTON	68,139	176,479
21	GEORGIA	58,910	152,576
22	FLORIDA	58,664	151,939
23	MICHIGAN	58,527	151,586
24	ILLINOIS	56,345	145,934
25	IOWA	56,275	145,753
26	WISCONSIN	56,153	145,436

*Area figures are from the *Statistical Abstract of the United States.*

27	ARKANSAS	53,187	137,754
28	NORTH CAROLINA	52,669	136,413
29	ALABAMA	51,705	133,915
30	NEW YORK	49,108	127,189
31	LOUISIANA	47,752	123,677
32	MISSISSIPPI	47,689	123,515
33	PENNSYLVANIA	45,308	117,348
34	TENNESSEE	42,144	109,152
35	OHIO	41,330	107,044
36	VIRGINIA	40,767	105,586
37	KENTUCKY	40,409	104,660
38	INDIANA	36,185	93,720
39	MAINE	33,265	86,156
40	SOUTH CAROLINA	31,113	80,582
41	WEST VIRGINIA	24,231	62,759
42	MARYLAND	10,460	27,092
43	VERMONT	9,614	24,900
44	NEW HAMPSHIRE	9,279	24,032
45	MASSACHUSETTS	8,284	21,456
46	NEW JERSEY	7,787	20,169
47	HAWAII	6,471	16,759
48	CONNECTICUT	5,018	12,997
49	DELAWARE	2,044	5,295
50	RHODE ISLAND	1,212	3,140

Total area of the United States: 3,618,770 square miles (9,372,614 sq km).

How do we find out about the number of people living in each of the fifty states?

The United States Bureau of the Census makes a count, called the census. The first census was taken in 1790, and there has been an official census every ten years since then—in 1800, 1810, 1820, and so on. In the years between the ten-year censuses, the Bureau of the Census makes an estimate of the population.

The following list shows each state's estimated population (rounded to the nearest thousand) and its rank on July 1, 1987. The estimated population of the United States at that time was 243,400,000. Each state's rank in area is also given so that you may compare the two rankings.

RANK		POPULATION*	RANK IN AREA
1	CALIFORNIA	27,663,000	3
2	NEW YORK	17,825,000	30
3	TEXAS	16,789,000	2
4	FLORIDA	12,023,000	22
5	PENNSYLVANIA	11,936,000	33
6	ILLINOIS	11,582,000	24
7	OHIO	10,784,000	35
8	MICHIGAN	9,200,000	23
9	NEW JERSEY	7,672,000	46
10	NORTH CAROLINA	6,413,000	28
11	GEORGIA	6,222,000	21
12	VIRGINIA	5,904,000	36
13	MASSACHUSETTS	5,855,000	45
14	INDIANA	5,531,000	38
15	MISSOURI	5,103,000	19
16	TENNESSEE	4,855,000	34
17	WISCONSIN	4,807,000	26
18	WASHINGTON	4,538,000	20
19	MARYLAND	4,535,000	42
20	LOUISIANA	4,461,000	31
21	MINNESOTA	4,246,000	12
22	ALABAMA	4,083,000	29
23	KENTUCKY	3,727,000	37
24	SOUTH CAROLINA	3,425,000	40
25	ARIZONA	3,386,000	6
26	COLORADO	3,296,000	8
27	OKLAHOMA	3,272,000	18
28	CONNECTICUT	3,211,000	48
29	IOWA	2,834,000	25
30	OREGON	2,724,000	10
31	MISSISSIPPI	2,625,000	32
32	KANSAS	2,476,000	14
33	ARKANSAS	2,388,000	27
34	WEST VIRGINIA	1,897,000	41
35	UTAH	1,680,000	11
36	NEBRASKA	1,594,000	15
37	NEW MEXICO	1,500,000	5
38	MAINE	1,187,000	39

*Population figures are always changing. As a state gains or loses in population, it may move up or down in rank. To find the latest facts about the population of the states and their rankings, look in the *Statistical Abstract of the United States*. Almanacs, such as the *World Almanac and Book of Facts*, also give information about population. New editions of these books are published each year.

39	HAWAII	1,083,000	47
40	NEW HAMPSHIRE	1,057,000	44
41	NEVADA	1,007,000	7
42	IDAHO	998,000	13
43	RHODE ISLAND	986,000	50
44	MONTANA	809,000	4
45	SOUTH DAKOTA	709,000	16
46	NORTH DAKOTA	672,000	17
47	DELAWARE	644,000	49
48	VERMONT	548,000	43
49	ALASKA	525,000	1
50	WYOMING	490,000	9

Arranging the states by rank in population makes it easy to see how each one compares with the others. You can also tell something about the parts of the country that have the most people. Here are some questions that you might answer (the map on pages 36 and 37 will help you answer some of them):

Which of the ten states that are largest in population are located along (or near) the Atlantic coast?

Which one among the first ten in population is along the Pacific coast?

Which ones of the first ten in population are along the Great Lakes?

How many of the states that rank from eleventh to twentieth in population are along the Atlantic coast (including the Gulf of Mexico) or along the Great Lakes?

States that are medium-sized in population have about how many people?

Which states are among the first ten both in population and in area?

Which one is among the first ten in population but among the last ten in area?

Which states are among the last ten both in population and in area?

The District of Columbia had about 626,000 people. Where would it rank if it were placed in the list with the states?

What Do the States Produce?

The United States, like other developed countries, produces three basic kinds of goods—agricultural (farm) products, minerals, and manufactured goods. Each state produces a share of each of these. But some states are known especially for farm products, others for minerals or manufacturing, and still others rank high in more than one kind of goods.

The nation's farms supply much of our food, as well as important raw materials (cotton, wool, and leather) from which clothing is made. What a state produces depends on its geography, especially soils and climate.

The following list shows the products that usually rank highest in value and the states that are the leading producers.*

CATTLE: Texas, Nebraska, Kansas, Iowa, Oklahoma
DAIRY PRODUCTS: Wisconsin, California, New York, Minnesota
SOYBEANS: Illinois, Iowa, Indiana, Minnesota, Ohio
CORN: Iowa, Illinois, Nebraska, Indiana, Minnesota
HOGS: Iowa, Illinois, Minnesota, Indiana, Nebraska
WHEAT: Kansas, North Dakota, Texas, Oklahoma, Washington

The states in the Central Lowland—from Ohio to eastern Kansas and Nebraska—make up one of the world's largest and richest agricultural regions. These states have deep, fertile soil, generally level land, and the kind of climate (warm, humid summers) in which corn grows best. They produce vast quantities of corn, soybeans, and other crops. Hogs and cattle also are raised here. The states in the Great Plains are famous for wheat and cattle. They have the kind of soil and

*Facts and figures about what each state produces, how much, and where it ranks among the fifty states—like population figures—change from year to year. To find the latest statistics (facts and figures), look in the *Statistical Abstract of the United States.* Most libraries have copies of this useful book, which is published each year. It contains information (mostly in the form of tables) about population of the states and their cities and metropolitan areas, geography (especially area, climate, and highest and lowest points), education, transportation, communications, forests, fisheries, agriculture, mining, manufacturing, and much more.

climate in which wheat thrives, as well as grasslands for pasturing cattle. Yet California, with its mountains and deserts, usually ranks first among the states in the dollar value of agricultural products sold each year. California has fertile valleys and a mild climate in which field crops, vegetables, and fruits can be grown year-round. Huge irrigation systems provide moisture.

Much of our food and some of our clothing come from materials on the surface of the earth. Trees, also on the surface, supply lumber for houses and furniture, and wood pulp for paper. But many other important products come from materials beneath the earth's surface. These materials are called minerals.

What a state produces depends on what minerals are beneath its surface. Mineral production also depends on what minerals are in demand. Recent years have brought an ever-increasing demand for the energy supplied by petroleum and natural gas. These mineral fuels, along with coal, also provide the chemicals from which plastics, synthetic fibers, fertilizers, and scores of other products are made. Concrete (made from cement and sand and gravel) also is in great demand for use in buildings and for paving streets and roads.

Could you guess which ones of the many minerals produced each year rank highest in value—and which states are among the leading producers? Here are the answers:

PETROLEUM: Texas, Alaska, Louisiana, California, Oklahoma
COAL: Kentucky, Wyoming, West Virginia, Pennsylvania
NATURAL GAS: Texas, Louisiana, Oklahoma, New Mexico
CEMENT: Texas, California, Pennsylvania, Michigan
COPPER: Arizona, New Mexico, Utah, Montana

Today more than 350,000 factories in the fifty states turn out some 10,000 different kinds of manufactured products—from ice cream and sneakers to bicycles and huge jet planes. One group of products that rank high in value is machinery. Without machines of many kinds, farmers and workers in mines and oil fields could not produce the raw materials that factories need. And factories could not operate without the many kinds of machines used to make products. Other groups of manufactured goods that rank high in value are foods (canned, frozen, and processed in other ways), transportation

Death Valley National Monument contains the lowest point in the Western Hemisphere.

equipment (cars and trucks, aircraft of various kinds, ships and boats), chemicals and chemical products, petroleum and coal products, and electric and electronic equipment.

Every state has factories, large or small. But the group of states stretching from New York and New Jersey westward to Illinois and Wisconsin leads all other areas in manufacturing. Other states that rank high in manufacturing include California and Texas. These states have large centers of population, which supply workers as well as a rich market for manufactured goods. The areas surrounding the cities produce many of the raw materials used in manufacturing. And all of these states have good land and water transportation for bringing in raw materials and sending out finished goods.

Conserving the States' Natural Wonders

What is the greatest natural wonder in the fifty states? Some people would say that the Grand Canyon of the Colorado River in Arizona is the most impressive and awe-inspiring. Others might choose Carlsbad Caverns in New Mexico, a huge glacier in Alaska, or fiery Kilauea Crater on the island of Hawaii. Still others would mention a grove of giant sequoias in California, the seashore of Cape Cod in Massachusetts, or the swampy wilderness of the Everglades in Florida.

Today these and many other places of natural beauty or historic or scientific interest are parts of national areas. These areas belong to all of the people of the United States. They are protected and managed for the people by agencies of the federal government. These areas now number in the hundreds, and the list is ever growing. They are classified according to kinds, such as national parks, monuments, historic places, forests, seashores, recreation areas, wild rivers, wildernesses, parkways, trails, and wildlife refuges. Each state also has a system of state areas, classified in much the same way as the national areas.

For our present system of national areas, we can thank a group of conservationists and naturalists of the late 1800s and early 1900s. They were concerned about the waste and destruction of our natural resources—forests, soil, water, grasslands, minerals, wildlife, and places of natural beauty.

The Native Americans can be called the first conservationists in North America. They took from the land only what they needed to live, and they wasted nothing. When settlers came from Europe, they found a land of seemingly endless resources. And they used those resources to the fullest. By the late 1800s, the country was on the way to becoming an industrial giant. Forests had been cut down. Parts of the countryside were scarred by mining. Rivers had been dammed for waterpower or polluted by wastes. Grasslands had been plowed up. Many wild creatures were in danger of disappearing because of uncontrolled killing or because their natural homes had been destroyed.

*At Craters of the Moon National Monument
in Idaho, volcanic cones, craters, lava
flows and caves create a fantastic landscape.*

It was high time to act, the conservationists said, so that future generations would have natural resources to use and places of natural beauty to enjoy. Yellowstone National Park, established in 1872, was the first national park in the United States, as well as in the world. The first national forest reserve (national forest) was set aside in Wyoming in 1891.

Do you know something (or maybe quite a bit) about your state's system of parks, forests, and other areas—and about the national areas, too? It is easy to get information. The department of parks in almost every state has folders and bulletins telling about both state and national areas. State highway departments issue colorful maps showing where these places are and how to reach them. To anyone who asks, the National Park and National Forest services send descriptions of all of the areas they manage, along with information about places to camp, hike, fish, and ski.

The work of conserving our resources—including our natural wonders—has not yet been completed. When you look around you, you see that the need to conserve resources and clean up our environment is greater than ever before. Each of us can help in this effort.

Which States Claim Presidents?

Which state claims the largest number of presidents?

VIRGINIA claims eight, the largest number. These presidents were born in Virginia (the number following each name tells which president the person was in numerical order):

George Washington, 1st

Thomas Jefferson, 3rd

James Madison, 4th

James Monroe, 5th

William Henry Harrison, 9th

John Tyler, 10th

Zachary Taylor, 12th

Woodrow Wilson, 28th

Which state ranks next in number of presidents born in the state?

OHIO is a close second to Virginia, with these seven presidents:

Ulysses S. Grant, 18th

Rutherford B. Hayes, 19th

James A. Garfield, 20th

Benjamin Harrison, 23rd

William McKinley, 25th

William Howard Taft, 27th

Warren G. Harding, 29th

Which state ranks third?

NEW YORK, which was the birthplace of these four presidents:

Martin Van Buren, 8th

Millard Fillmore, 13th

Theodore Roosevelt, 26th

Franklin D. Roosevelt, 32nd

Which state is next?

MASSACHUSETTS, with three presidents:

John Adams, 2nd

John Quincy Adams, 6th

John F. Kennedy, 35th

Which states have been the birthplace of two presidents each?

NORTH CAROLINA:	James K. Polk, 11th
	Andrew Johnson, 17th
TEXAS:	Dwight D. Eisenhower, 34th
	Lyndon B. Johnson, 36th
VERMONT:	Chester A. Arthur, 21st
	Calvin Coolidge, 30th

Which states claim one president each?

CALIFORNIA:	Richard M. Nixon, 37th
GEORGIA:	Jimmy (James Earl) Carter, 39th
IOWA:	Herbert Hoover, 31st
ILLINOIS:	Ronald Reagan, 40th
KENTUCKY:	Abraham Lincoln, 16th
MISSOURI:	Harry S. Truman, 33rd
NEBRASKA:	Gerald R. Ford, 38th
NEW HAMPSHIRE:	Franklin Pierce, 14th
NEW JERSEY:	Grover Cleveland, 22nd and 24th
PENNSYLVANIA:	James Buchanan, 15th
SOUTH CAROLINA:	Andrew Jackson, 7th*

* Andrew Jackson was born in Waxhaw, a backwoods settlement on the border between South Carolina and North Carolina, and both states claim the site of the settlement. President Jackson considered South Carolina his birthplace.

Which States Claim Vice-Presidents?

As a birthplace of vice-presidents of the United States, New York is the leader by far, with eight. Kentucky is next, followed by Ohio and Vermont.

In the following list, the number after the name tells which vice-president the person was in numerical order. The name of the person who was president at the time is shown in parentheses.

CALIFORNIA: Richard M. Nixon, 36th (Eisenhower)

INDIANA: Thomas R. Marshall, 28th (Wilson)

IOWA: Henry A. Wallace, 33rd (F. D. Roosevelt)

KANSAS: Charles Curtis, 31st (Hoover)

KENTUCKY: Richard M. Johnson, 9th (Van Buren)
John C. Breckinridge, 14th (Buchanan)
Adlai E. Stevenson, 23rd (Cleveland)
Alben W. Barkley, 35th (Truman)

MAINE: Hannibal Hamlin, 15th (Lincoln)
Nelson A. Rockefeller, 41st (Ford)

MARYLAND: Spiro T. Agnew, 39th (Nixon)

MASSACHUSETTS: John Adams, 1st (Washington)
Elbridge Gerry, 5th (Madison)
George H. W. Bush, 43rd (Reagan)

MINNESOTA: Walter F. Mondale, 42nd (Carter)

MISSOURI: Harry S. Truman, 34th (F. D. Roosevelt)

NEBRASKA: Gerald R. Ford, 40th (Nixon)

NEW HAMPSHIRE: Henry Wilson, 18th (Grant)

NEW JERSEY: Aaron Burr, 3rd (Jefferson)
Garret A. Hobart, 24th (McKinley)

NEW YORK: George Clinton, 4th (Jefferson and Madison)
Daniel D. Tompkins, 6th (Monroe)

Martin Van Buren, 8th (Jackson)
Millard Fillmore, 12th (Taylor)
Schuyler Colfax, 17th (Grant)
William A. Wheeler, 19th (Hayes)
Theodore Roosevelt, 25th (McKinley)
James S. Sherman, 27th (Taft)

NORTH CAROLINA: William R. King, 13th (Pierce)
                    Andrew Johnson, 16th (Lincoln)

OHIO: Thomas A. Hendricks, 21st (Cleveland)
                    Charles W. Fairbanks, 26th (T. Roosevelt)
                    Charles G. Dawes, 30th (Coolidge)

PENNSYLVANIA: George M. Dallas, 11th (Polk)

SOUTH CAROLINA: John C. Calhoun, 7th (J. Q. Adams and Jackson)

SOUTH DAKOTA   Hubert H. Humphrey, 38th (L. B. Johnson)

TEXAS: John N. Garner, 32nd (F. D. Roosevelt)
                    Lyndon B. Johnson, 37th (Kennedy)

VERMONT: Chester A. Arthur, 20th (Garfield)
                    Levi P. Morton, 22nd (B. Harrison)
                    Calvin Coolidge, 29th (Harding)

VIRGINIA: Thomas Jefferson, 2nd (J. Adams)
                    John Tyler, 10th (W. H. Harrison)

Who Was Who? Presidential Trivia

You can find the answers to the first fourteen questions below by studying the table on the next page. Answers to the other questions are on page 60.

1. Do you have the same birth month and day as a president of the United States?
2. What two presidents died on the Fourth of July in the same year?
3. What other president died on the Fourth of July?
4. What president was born on the Fourth of July?
5. Which president was the youngest when he was inaugurated (took the oath of office as president)?
6. Which president was the oldest when inaugurated?
7. William Henry Harrison was inaugurated on March 4, 1841. How long did he serve as president?
8. Franklin D. Roosevelt was president from his first inauguration (on March 4, 1933) until his death. How long did he serve?
9. What president served one term (four years), was followed by another president, and then was elected president again?
10. Who was president during the Civil War (1861–1865)?
11. Who served as president during World War I (1914–1918)?
12. Who was president during World War II (1939–1945)?
13. What presidents lived to the oldest age?
14. What presidents had the same last name?
15. Which presidents were father and son?
16. Which ones were grandfather and grandson?
17. Were the other presidents with the same last name related to each other?
18. What president became vice-president and then president without having been elected to those offices by the people?
19. Which presidents died while in office?
20. How many vice-presidents became president?

More Presidential Facts

No.	Name	Born	Inaug.	Age	Died	Age
1	George Washington	1732, Feb. 22	1789	57	1799, Dec. 14	67
2	John Adams	1735, Oct. 30	1797	61	1826, July 4	90
3	Thomas Jefferson	1743, Apr. 13	1801	57	1826, July 4	83
4	James Madison	1751, Mar. 16	1809	57	1836, June 28	85
5	James Monroe	1758, Apr. 28	1817	58	1831, July 4	73
6	John Quincy Adams	1767, July 11	1825	57	1848, Feb. 23	80
7	Andrew Jackson	1767, Mar. 15	1829	61	1845, June 8	78
8	Martin Van Buren	1782, Dec. 5	1837	54	1862, July 24	79
9	William Henry Harrison	1773, Feb. 9	1841	68	1841, Apr. 4	68
10	John Tyler	1790, Mar. 29	1841	51	1862, Jan. 18	71
11	James Knox Polk	1795, Nov. 2	1845	49	1849, June 15	53
12	Zachary Taylor	1784, Nov. 24	1849	64	1850, July 9	65
13	Millard Fillmore	1800, Jan. 7	1850	50	1874, Mar. 8	74
14	Franklin Pierce	1804, Nov. 23	1853	48	1869, Oct. 8	64
15	James Buchanan	1791, Apr. 23	1857	65	1868, June 1	77
16	Abraham Lincoln	1809, Feb. 12	1861	52	1865, Apr. 15	56
17	Andrew Johnson	1808, Dec. 29	1865	56	1875, July 31	66
18	Ulysses Simpson Grant	1822, Apr. 27	1869	46	1885, July 23	63
19	Rutherford Birchard Hayes	1822, Oct. 4	1877	54	1893, Jan. 17	70
20	James Abram Garfield	1831, Nov. 19	1881	49	1881, Sept. 19	49
21	Chester Alan Arthur	1829, Oct. 5	1881	51	1886, Nov. 18	57
22	Grover Cleveland	1837, Mar. 18	1885	47	1908, June 24	71
23	Benjamin Harrison	1833, Aug. 20	1889	55	1901, Mar. 13	67
24	Grover Cleveland	1837, Mar. 18	1893	55	1908, June 24	71
25	William McKinley	1843, Jan. 29	1897	54	1901, Sept. 14	58
26	Theodore Roosevelt	1858, Oct. 27	1901	42	1919, Jan. 6	60
27	William Howard Taft	1857, Sept. 15	1909	51	1930, Mar. 8	72
28	(Thomas) Woodrow Wilson	1856, Dec. 28	1913	56	1924, Feb. 3	67
29	Warren Gamaliel Harding	1865, Nov. 2	1921	55	1923, Aug. 2	57
30	(John) Calvin Coolidge	1872, July 4	1923	51	1933, Jan. 5	60
31	Herbert Clark Hoover	1874, Aug. 10	1929	54	1964, Oct. 20	90
32	Franklin Delano Roosevelt	1882, Jan. 30	1933	51	1945, Apr. 12	63
33	Harry S. Truman	1884, May 8	1945	60	1972, Dec. 26	88
34	Dwight David Eisenhower	1890, Oct. 14	1953	62	1969, Mar. 28	78
35	John Fitzgerald Kennedy	1917, May 29	1961	43	1963, Nov. 22	46
36	Lyndon Baines Johnson	1908, Aug. 27	1963	55	1973, Jan. 22	64
37	Richard Milhous Nixon	1913, Jan. 9	1969	56		
38	Gerald Rudolph Ford	1913, July 14	1974	61		
39	Jimmy (James Earl) Carter	1924, Oct. 1	1977	52		
40	Ronald Wilson Reagan	1911, Feb. 6	1981	69		

ANSWERS TO QUESTIONS ON PAGE 58:

15. John Adams was the father of John Quincy Adams.
16. William Henry Harrison was the grandfather of Benjamin Harrison.
17. Andrew Johnson and Lyndon B. Johnson were not related. Theodore Roosevelt was a distant cousin of Franklin D. Roosevelt.
18. Gerald R. Ford (a member of the U.S. House of Representatives) was named vice-president by President Richard M. Nixon after Vice-President Spiro T. Agnew resigned in 1973. Ford became president when Nixon resigned in 1974.
19. Eight presidents have died in office. Four died of natural causes —William Henry Harrison, Zachary Taylor, Warren G. Harding, and Franklin D. Roosevelt. Four were assassinated—Abraham Lincoln, James Garfield, William McKinley, and John F. Kennedy.
20. Thirteen vice-presidents became presidents:

John Adams	Theodore Roosevelt
Thomas Jefferson	Calvin Coolidge
Martin Van Buren	Harry S. Truman
John Tyler	Lyndon B. Johnson
Millard Fillmore	Richard M. Nixon
Andrew Johnson	Gerald R. Ford
Chester A. Arthur	

What's in a Nickname?

Why is New York called the Empire State?

It is thought that the idea for the nickname came from a speech made by George Washington in 1785, in which he referred to New York as "at present the seat of Empire." (New York City served as the seat of the national government—the national capital—from 1785 to 1790.)

Who's a Hoosier?

A Hoosier is an Indianan. This is the nickname of both the state and the people. No one knows exactly where this name came from or how Indiana acquired it, but it is one of the best known of all the state nicknames.

Which state is the Show-Me State?

That's Missouri. Although no one knows the exact origin of this nickname, either, almost everyone knows the saying, "I'm from Missouri, and you'll have to show me."

Why is Colorado called the Centennial State?

This nickname comes from the fact that Colorado became a state in 1876—the centennial (100th anniversary) of the signing of the Declaration of Independence.

All the other states have nicknames, too. Some have more than one, and some have had several during their histories. The present nicknames of the rest of the states are given in the following list.

ALABAMA: Heart of Dixie
ALASKA: The Great Land; Last Frontier
ARIZONA: Grand Canyon State
ARKANSAS: Land of Opportunity
CALIFORNIA: Golden State
CONNECTICUT: Constitution State
DELAWARE: First State
FLORIDA: Sunshine State
GEORGIA: Empire State of the South; Peach State

*A mighty glacier, or stream of ice, flows
from two sides to surround a mountain peak at
Glacier Bay National Park, Alaska.*

HAWAII: Aloha State
IDAHO: Gem State
ILLINOIS: Prairie State; Land of Lincoln
IOWA: Hawkeye State
KANSAS: Sunflower State
KENTUCKY: Bluegrass State
LOUISIANA: Pelican State
MAINE: Pine Tree State
MARYLAND: Old Line State
MASSACHUSETTS: Bay State
MICHIGAN: Wolverine State
MINNESOTA: North Star State
MISSISSIPPI: Magnolia State
MONTANA: Treasure State
NEBRASKA: Cornhusker State
NEVADA: Silver State
NEW HAMPSHIRE: Granite State
NEW JERSEY: Garden State
NEW MEXICO: Land of Enchantment
NORTH CAROLINA: Tar Heel State; Old North State
NORTH DAKOTA: Flickertail State; Sioux State; Peace Garden State
OHIO: Buckeye State
OKLAHOMA: Sooner State
OREGON: Beaver State
PENNSYLVANIA: Keystone State
RHODE ISLAND: Little Rhody
SOUTH CAROLINA: Palmetto State
SOUTH DAKOTA: Coyote State; Sunshine State
TENNESSEE: Volunteer State
TEXAS: Lone Star State
UTAH: Beehive State
VERMONT: Green Mountain State
VIRGINIA: Old Dominion
WASHINGTON: Evergreen State
WEST VIRGINIA: Mountain State
WISCONSIN: Badger State
WYOMING: Equality State; Cowboy State

Why Have Symbols and Emblems?

Why do the states and the United States, too, have flags, seals, mottoes, birds, flowers, and other emblems?*

One definition of the word "nation," "country," or "state" is "a body of people politically organized and occupying a certain territory." We can see how this definition applies to both the states and the nation. First of all, there must be people. Then the people must have a certain area of land that they call their own, and they must have a government under which they live.

One of the first things that the founders (the people who help to establish, or found, a country or a state) do is to choose a name. The name establishes the identity of the state or country and helps to give it a "personality."

Then the founders design a flag, using colors and symbols that have special meaning for the people. The flag becomes the main emblem of the state or country. Usually the founders choose a motto—a word, phrase, or sentence (often in Latin) that helps express the "character" of the country or state and gives the people a principle, or important idea, to guide their lives.

The founders usually give careful thought to the design of at least one other emblem—the state or national seal, often called the "great seal." The seal becomes the "signature" of the state or nation, and it is placed on all official documents. Most of the states have their motto on the state seal.

*It would take many pages to show and explain the details of all of the flags and seals of the fifty states. The designs tell much about the history and traditions of each state. The articles on the states in *The New Book of Knowledge* and other encyclopedias give information about the state emblems. Too, most states have special leaflets or booklets explaining or listing all of their emblems and symbols. These can be obtained by writing to the secretary of state in each state.

*The State Flag of Louisiana and
the Great Seal of the State of New York*

Each state also has a bird, flower, and tree, and most have several other symbols that help express the personality of the state and tell something important or unusual about it. Many of the emblems and symbols are official—that is, they have been adopted by acts of the state legislature. In many instances, the schoolchildren of a state have helped to choose some of them.

The state birds, flowers, and trees are listed on pages 66 and 67. Here are examples of other kinds of state symbols:

ANIMAL: horse, dog, bear, beaver, coyote, raccoon, badger
INSECT: honeybee, ladybug, butterfly, firefly, praying mantis
MINERAL: hematite, gold, fluorite, beryl, silver
GEM OR GEMSTONE: jade, turquoise, diamond, agate, garnet
GRASS: bluebunch wheatgrass, western wheatgrass, little bluestem
DANCE: square dance, shag
BEVERAGE: orange juice, cranberry juice, tomato juice, milk
FISH: tarpon, cod, king salmon, striped bass, largemouth bass, humuhumunu-
    kunukuapuaa*

*This is the state fish of Hawaii. It is one of a kind of fish known in English as triggerfish. To pronounce the Hawaiian name, first divide it into syllables (hu-mu-hu-mu-nu-ku-nu-ku-a-pu-a-a). Then say it this way (the double *o*'s are pronounced as in "too"): hoo' muh hoo' muh noo' kuh noo' kuh ah' poo' ah' wah.

STATE	BIRD	FLOWER	TREE
Alabama	Yellowhammer	Camelia	Longleaf pine
Alaska	Willow ptarmigan	Forget-me-not	Sitka spruce
Arizona	Cactus wren	Saguaro cactus blossom	Paloverde
Arkansas	Mockingbird	Apple blossom	Shortleaf pine
California	California valley quail	Golden poppy	California redwood
Colorado	Lark bunting	Rocky Mountain columbine	Colorado blue spruce
Connecticut	American robin	Mountain laurel	White oak
Delaware	Blue hen chicken	Peach blossom	American holly
Florida	Mockingbird	Orange blossom	Cabbage palmetto
Georgia	Brown thrasher	Cherokee rose	Live oak
Hawaii	Nene (Hawaiian goose)	Red hibiscus	Kukui (candlenut tree)
Idaho	Mountain bluebird	Syringa	Western white pine
Illinois	Eastern cardinal	Violet	White oak
Indiana	Cardinal	Peony	Tulip tree
Iowa	Eastern goldfinch	Wild rose	Oak
Kansas	Western meadowlark	Sunflower	Cottonwood
Kentucky	Cardinal	Goldenrod	Kentucky coffee tree
Louisiana	Eastern brown pelican	Magnolia	Bald cypress
Maine	Chickadee	Eastern white pine cone and tassel	Eastern white pine
Maryland	Baltimore oriole	Black-eyed Susan	White oak
Massachusetts	Chickadee	Mayflower	American elm
Michigan	Robin	Apple blossom	Eastern white pine
Minnesota	Loon	Showy (pink-and-white) lady's slipper	Red (Norway) pine

STATE	BIRD	FLOWER	TREE
Mississippi	Mockingbird	Magnolia blossom	Southern magnolia
Missouri	Bluebird	Hawthorn	Flowering dogwood
Montana	Western meadowlark	Bitterroot	Ponderosa pine
Nebraska	Western meadowlark	Goldenrod	Cottonwood
Nevada	Mountain bluebird	Sagebrush	Single-leaf pinyon
New Hampshire	Purple finch	Purple lilac	Paper birch
New Jersey	Eastern goldfinch	Purple violet	Red oak
New Mexico	Roadrunner	Yucca	Pinyon
New York	Bluebird	Rose	Sugar maple
North Carolina	Cardinal	Dogwood	Pine
North Dakota	Western meadowlark	Wild prairie rose	American elm
Ohio	Cardinal	Scarlet carnation	Buckeye
Oklahoma	Scissor-tailed flycatcher	Mistletoe	Redbud
Oregon	Western meadowlark	Oregon grape	Douglas fir
Pennsylvania	Ruffed grouse	Mountain laurel	Eastern hemlock
Rhode Island	Rhode Island Red	Violet	Red maple
South Carolina	Carolina wren	Yellow jasmine	Palmetto
South Dakota	Ring-necked pheasant	Pasqueflower	White spruce
Tennessee	Mockingbird	Iris	Yellow poplar
Texas	Mockingbird	Bluebonnet	Pecan
Utah	Sea gull	Sego lily	Blue spruce
Vermont	Hermit thrush	Red clover	Sugar maple
Virginia	Cardinal	Flowering dogwood	Dogwood
Washington	Willow goldfinch	Coast rhododendron	Western hemlock
West Virginia	Cardinal	Great rhododendron	Sugar maple
Wisconsin	Robin	Violet	Sugar maple
Wyoming	Western meadowlark	Indian paintbrush	Cottonwood

Capitals and Biggest Cities

Is the capital of your state also the largest city? In how many states is the capital the largest city? The following lists give the answers. You can use the lists to test yourself or someone else on state capitals. If you are testing yourself, cover the capitals or the states with a strip of paper.

STATE	CAPITAL	LARGEST CITY
ALABAMA	MONTGOMERY	BIRMINGHAM
ALASKA	JUNEAU	ANCHORAGE
ARIZONA	PHOENIX	PHOENIX
ARKANSAS	LITTLE ROCK	LITTLE ROCK
CALIFORNIA	SACRAMENTO	LOS ANGELES
COLORADO	DENVER	DENVER
CONNECTICUT	HARTFORD	BRIDGEPORT
DELAWARE	DOVER	WILMINGTON
FLORIDA	TALLAHASSEE	JACKSONVILLE
GEORGIA	ATLANTA	ATLANTA
HAWAII	HONOLULU	HONOLULU
IDAHO	BOISE	BOISE
ILLINOIS	SPRINGFIELD	CHICAGO
INDIANA	INDIANAPOLIS	INDIANAPOLIS
IOWA	DES MOINES	DES MOINES
KANSAS	TOPEKA	WICHITA
KENTUCKY	FRANKFORT	LOUISVILLE
LOUISIANA	BATON ROUGE	NEW ORLEANS
MAINE	AUGUSTA	PORTLAND
MARYLAND	ANNAPOLIS	BALTIMORE
MASSACHUSETTS	BOSTON	BOSTON
MICHIGAN	LANSING	DETROIT
MINNESOTA	SAINT PAUL	MINNEAPOLIS
MISSISSIPPI	JACKSON	JACKSON
MISSOURI	JEFFERSON CITY	ST. LOUIS
MONTANA	HELENA	BILLINGS
NEBRASKA	LINCOLN	OMAHA

STATE	CAPITAL	LARGEST CITY
NEVADA	CARSON CITY	LAS VEGAS
NEW HAMPSHIRE	CONCORD	MANCHESTER
NEW JERSEY	TRENTON	NEWARK
NEW MEXICO	SANTA FE	ALBUQUERQUE
NEW YORK	ALBANY	NEW YORK
NORTH CAROLINA	RALEIGH	CHARLOTTE
NORTH DAKOTA	BISMARCK	FARGO
OHIO	COLUMBUS	COLUMBUS*
OKLAHOMA	OKLAHOMA CITY	OKLAHOMA CITY
OREGON	SALEM	PORTLAND
PENNSYLVANIA	HARRISBURG	PHILADELPHIA
RHODE ISLAND	PROVIDENCE	PROVIDENCE
SOUTH CAROLINA	COLUMBIA	COLUMBIA
SOUTH DAKOTA	PIERRE	SIOUX FALLS
TENNESSEE	NASHVILLE	MEMPHIS
TEXAS	AUSTIN	HOUSTON
UTAH	SALT LAKE CITY	SALT LAKE CITY
VERMONT	MONTPELIER	BURLINGTON
VIRGINIA	RICHMOND	NORFOLK
WASHINGTON	OLYMPIA	SEATTLE
WEST VIRGINIA	CHARLESTON	CHARLESTON
WISCONSIN	MADISON	MILWAUKEE
WYOMING	CHEYENNE	CASPER

*Census estimates during the 1980s showed that Columbus moved into first place, ahead of Cleveland.

Index

973
B

Brandt, Sue R.

Facts about the
fifty states

$10.40

DATE		

© THE BAKER & TAYLOR CO.